Despite providing glorious walking, the heath is easily over
to Purbeck drive straight across it, eager to reach Corfe Cast
the heathland tucked into this corner of Dorset is renowned
of Britain's most fragile habitat, supporting a wealth of plants and animals, many
of them scarce. Some of the heath is dry and sandy. Elsewhere there are bogs and
pools. Creeks and mud flats line the shore of Poole Harbour.

The hills divide the heath from the rest of Purbeck. Beginning at Old Harry's
chalk stack off Handfast Point they climb steadily, gradually widening behind
Lulworth Cove and Durdle Door. Their only interruption is the most famous of
all Purbeck's landmarks – the dramatic silhouette of Corfe Castle, which crowns
the one gap in the ridge. This is a Conqueror's castle, built by William I and
strengthened and added to by successive medieval monarchs, for whom Purbeck
was a royal hunting preserve. Corfe's summer crowds, and the cheerful whistle
of the steam engines on the Swanage Railway, give way to farmland that

stretches from the resort town of Swanage to Tyneham, the abandoned village now in the centre of an Army firing range. Swanage's architectural treasure trove and half-moon of sand have given it a character uniquely its own. Much of the surrounding countryside is rich grassland. Ancient trackways link lovely stone manor houses and farmhouses, skirting copses awash with wild flowers.

The green of the Wealden valley is a far cry from the land running south to the sea. This is stone country, raw and wild, whose origins date back to the birth of the Jurassic period, 140 million years ago. Dorset was then positioned at about the latitude of the Mediterranean and its climate was that of the Red Sea. Fossilised dinosaur footprints have been found, as well as crocodiles, hippopotami and turtles. Limestone quarries scar the windswept coastal plateau. Purbeck marble was first quarried by the Romans, and throughout the Middle Ages was used to decorate churches all over England. The limestone beds were worked for building stone, roofing slates and dry-stone walling. Old quarry workings are everywhere, and can best seen on the coast, where the cliff path running the length of Purbeck makes for some of the finest coastal walking in Britain.

Looking up the River Frome towards Wareham. The town is 12 miles from the sea, but boats still ply up the winding tidal river to moor alongside the quay in its centre. In Saxon times it was one of Dorset's most important fortified towns, but the rise of Poole, the gradual silting of the Frome, and the increase in ships' sizes ended its days as a port. Happily it is now bypassed, which together with the remaining ramparts has helped preserve its charm.

ABOVE Wareham Quay and the River Frome.

RIGHT St Martin's, Wareham, sits astride the defensive walls thrown up by King Alfred to keep the Vikings at bay near the site of the old north gate into the town. As well as being the most complete Saxon church in Dorset, St Martin's also includes some lovely 12th century frescoes telling the story of the saint's conversion.

BELOW The effigy of T.E. Lawrence (of Arabia) by Eric Kennington in St Martin's Church, Wareham. Lawrence is shown in Arab dress, with his head resting on a camel's saddle bag. Lawrence retired to his cottage at Bovington after he left the Air Force in 1935, and was killed in a motorbike accident a few months later.

ABOVE The 15th century Holme Bridge over the River Piddle, near Wareham. The bridge has been extended and repaired several times over the centuries, and is famous as the scene of a Civil War skirmish between 300 'rebels' and a force from the Royalist garrison in Wareham in which 40 rebels were killed. The old stone parapets were damaged by tanks training during the Second World War and have been replaced by brick.

LEFT Pine trees fringe the Blue Pool, Furzebrook. The 50 feet deep pool owes its name to tiny particles of clay suspended in the water which refraction has the effect of making appear blue. It was dug for its clay in the 1840s, when Purbeck ball-clay was in demand for everything from clay tobacco pipes to fine Wedgwood china, and has been a popular tourist attraction since the 1930s.

LEFT Ancient oaks in Kilwood Nature Reserve, near the Blue Pool. Once an area of clay mining, dating back to Roman times, the 40 acre Dorset Wildlife Trust reserve has gradually regenerated, creating a mixture of wildlife rich birch and oak woodland, grassland and ponds.

ABOVE Godlingston Heath. Virtually the entire area between Corfe Castle and Wareham is open heathland. Once rough-grazing for livestock, as well as providing fuel in the form of peat and gorse, the Dorset heath is now regarded as the most precious of all its habitats. Some areas are dry, given over to heather and bracken, others are boggier with scattered pools. As a result, the heath boasts a wonderful wildlife.

RIGHT The cairn on Stoborough Heath, near Ridge, commemorating the formation of the 109 hectare National Nature Reserve in 1985. Together with the neighbouring 243 hectares of Hartland Moor, Stoborough is a mixture of dry heathland and valley bog draining into Poole Harbour. Once it was much given over to grassland, but the gradual reinstatement of the heath by cutting gorse and scrub has enriched the flora and provided the right habitat for nesting birds, reptiles and insects – many of them very rare.

Riding on the heath behind Studland village.

The simple medieval church at Arne. The church has no electricity, and is dedicated to St Nicholas of Myra, patron saint of sailors, and dates to a time when the small heathland village stood on the route to the quays on the west side of Poole Harbour. The village was evacuated during the Second World War, and badly damaged after decoy beacons were lit on the Arne peninsula to draw enemy bombers away from Poole and the Royal Naval Cordite Factory at Holton Heath. The photograph on the right shows the church decorated for the annual Flower Festival.

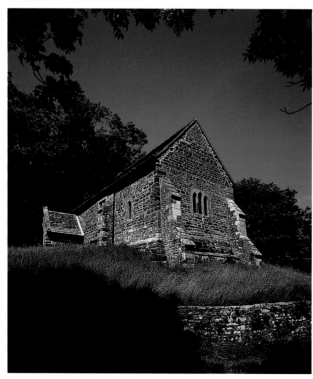

Studland Bay from Ballard Down, with a cross-Channel ferry bound for Cherbourg making its way out to sea.

Knoll Beach, Studland. With its sheltered shallow waters, clean sand, and easy access, the lovely curve of beach at Studland is one of the most accessible in Dorset.

The Agglestone on Godlingstone Heath, with Studland Bay and the Bournemouth skyline in the background. The 500 ton block of sandstone was supposedly thrown by the Devil from the Isle of Wight at Corfe Castle in a moment of anger. It fell short, and now forms an unusual feature on the heath.

Studland Cross. The heathstone base long ago lost its ancient village cross, and in 1976 the marbler Treleven Haysom carved a new one from a piece of stone from St Aldhelm's Quarry, mixing traditional designs with new ones of such things as 'Spaceship Earth'.

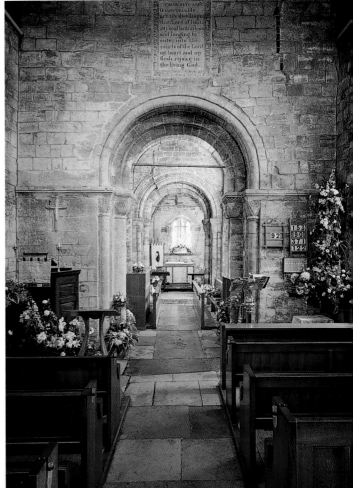

ABOVE RIGHT AND RIGHT The church of St Nicholas, Studland, is one of the finest Norman churches in the country – though there are still fragments of an earlier Saxon building largely destroyed by the Vikings during one of their many raids into Purbeck.

The photograph on the right shows the warm honey-coloured stone of the Norman arches leading into the choir and chancel.

There is much of interest, including the other-wordly carved animal and human heads on the outside where the stone roof meets the wall of the nave. There is also a wonderful memorial in the churchyard to Sergeant William Lawrence, a veteran of Waterloo who returned to Dorset to run an inn in Studland with his French bride, Clotilde.

Sunrise over Handfast Point and the chalk stack of Old Harry, and the reverse view from the sea.

ABOVE Swanage from Ballard Down, with the long arm of Peveril Point protecting the town from south-westerly gales. Until the arrival of the railway in 1885 Swanage was a small port best known for the shipping of building stone and decorative 'marble' from the local quarries.

RIGHT Punch and Judy on the beach at Swanage.

BELOW Holidaymakers gathered to watch the parade of floats at Swanage Carnival, which traditionally finishes with a display by the Royal Air Force air acrobatic team, the Red Arrows.

ABOVE The spring-fed millpond, Church Hill, Swanage. The town's oldest buildings lie well inland. In the background is the medieval tower of St Mary's church. Just above the clock you can see where it was heightened in 1620 to make it more visible as a waymark for shipping.

What makes Swanage such a delight to wander round is the architectural bric-a-brac brought back to it by George Burt, head of the firm of building contractors founded by his uncle John Mowlem. Amongst them (ABOVE LEFT) are the classical central façade of the Town Hall, which came from the Mercer's Hall in London, and (BELOW LEFT) the Wellington Clock Tower on Peveril Point, which began life as a memorial to the Duke of Wellington at one end of London Bridge.

The 40 ton Portland stone Globe at Durlston Country Park, Swanage. Another of Burt's whims, the Globe is surrounded by slabs bearing improving quotations as well as some left blank for intending graffiti artists: 'Persons anxious to write their names will do so on this stone only'.

Anvil Point lighthouse was built in 1881 where a Telegraph and Signal Station already stood and has a range of 24 miles. It was fully automated in 1991, and its 1000 watt lamp has the strength of 500,000 candles. The Purbeck coast is notorious for the races off its headlands, specially when wind and tide are opposed, and the lighthouse provides a valuable waypoint for coastal shipping.

BELOW Dancing Ledge. The pool on the ledge was blasted out of the cliff quarry shelf as a swimming pool in 1893 for the pupils of Durnford House School, a now long-closed boys prep school in Langton Matravers. There is a footpath down to the ledge along Durnford Drove, and another off the Priest's Way near Spyway Barn.

BELOW The old quarry workings at Tilly Whim Caves, between Durlston Head and Anvil Point. The workings extended in galleries some 200 feet into the hillside, and take their name from the whim, a sturdy wooden derrick used to lower the blocks of stone into barges, from where they were taken to larger ships waiting offshore or to Swanage Quay.

ABOVE Thrift in flower at Seacombe. The blue skies and calm seas are deceptive. It was here in 1786 that a 785 ton East Indiaman, the *Halsewell* struck the cliff in the middle of a bitterly cold January night. By the time the alarm had been raised and local quarriers had finished hauling the survivors to safety, the death toll had risen to 166, seven of them young women being sent to India in hope of attracting husbands. Many years later Charles Dickens turned the tragedy into a short story called 'The Long Voyage'.

RIGHT Winter on the Priest's Way. Until the 16th century this ancient track was used by the priest at Worth Matravers for his weekly journey to Swanage, which then only had a small chapel. It makes for a splendid fairly level three mile walk, with wonderful views out to sea.

ABOVE The old quarry workings at Winspit.

RIGHT The Square and Compass, Worth Matravers. Famous for its Fossil Museum, live music, guest beers and ciders, the pub has been run by the Newman family for over a century. The name comes from the tools used for marking out stone.

BELOW St Aldhelm's Chapel. One legend ascribes the construction of the Norman chapel to a local squire who, after witnessing his newly married daughter and her bridegroom being drowned in the notorious race of St Aldhelm's Head, built the Chapel as a chantry where masses were sung for the drowned and whose roof could support a warning beacon.

St Aldhelm's Quarry, Worth Matravers. The beds of Portland Freestone are still quarried for building stone.

Cottages at Worth Matravers built of local Purbeck limestone. Stone from the thinner beds in the quarries has long been used for roofing. They are much heavier than slates or tiles, so the largest are laid near the eaves and the smallest at the apex of the roof – originally on a bed of moss.

During the Second World War a radar station was established near Worth Matravers. Still visible on St Aldhelm's Head are the clifftop remains of one site, established in 1940 to allow the detection of aircraft flying as low as 500 feet at a distance of 25 miles, and it is near here that the Radar Memorial was unveiled in 2001. Also on the headland were two 240 feet high wooden radar towers, and an airstrip known as RAF Worth Matravers which was opened to serve the needs of the scientific community based at the radar station. In the background is the National Coastguard lookout, now manned by volunteers who keep a watchful eye on yachts and fishing boats rounding St Aldhelm's Head.

OPPOSITE PAGE The coastal footpath between St Aldhelm's Head and Emmetts Hill is deceptively steep, and few but the fittest walkers don't pause for breath before reaching either summit. The heights of Houns Tout frame the background.

ABOVE Chapman's Pool, with the stone heights of Emmetts Hill rising up over the eroded tumble of undercliff and the huddle of fishermen's huts on the eastern shore. The bay can be used as an anchorage only in the most settled weather, for there is scant shelter from the open sea. The coastguard cottages on St Aldhelm's Head are visible in the background on the right.

RIGHT Looking west from Houns Tout, 500 feet above the sea below. The word 'tout' means 'look-out' and it is easy to see why. Peregrine falcons can occasionally be seen hunting over the undercliff below.

A tiny stream known as the South Gwyle runs from the lakes at Encombe House, finally cascading over the cliff at Egmont Bight.

Of all Dorset's great houses, Encombe surely enjoys the most spectacular setting. Sitting at the head of what is known as the Golden Bowl, the long stone mansion was built by John Pitt, a cousin of William Pitt, the great 18th century Prime Minister. Thanks to his wife's extravagance, John Scott's son Morton was forced to sell both house and estate to John Scott, later the Lord Chancellor and 1st Earl of Eldon, in whose family it remained until about twenty years ago. Visible on the left is the obelisk erected by the 1st Earl in memory of his brother. Not visible in the photograph are the lakes in the bowl of the valley, which gave the illusion that the sea laps almost to the front of the house.

St James, Kingston. Known as
the 'cathedral of the Purbecks',
the church was built by the 3rd
Earl of Eldon in memory of his
grandfather, the Lord Chancellor.
The church was started in about
1873 and was designed by G.E.
Street, whose work includes the
Law Courts in London. St James
is generally regarded as one of the
finest of all Victorian churches, and
the interior is an exquisite medley
of Purbeck marble, fine carving,
wrought iron work and stained
glass.

ABOVE Corfe Castle and village. The ruined Castle is Dorset's most famous landmark. Nothing remains of the Saxon building near which Edward the Martyr was murdered at the order of his step-mother in 978. The present Castle was begun by William the Conqueror shortly after the Norman invasion, and was strengthened and added to throughout the Middle Ages. The Castle was never a permanent royal residence, but its strategic importance on the only gap in the Purbeck Hills was significant, and monarchs stayed in it when travelling round the kingdom.

LEFT The Castle from the west. The two ruined walls rising from the summit were part of the 13th century Keep, which contained the King's Hall and the royal apartments.

A reconstruction of the most famous episode in the Castle's history, the Civil War siege when it was held for the king by Lady Bankes, wife of the owner. With a garrison of five men and handful of maids, 'Brave Dame Mary' resisted a siege in 1643, only to be forced to surrender three years later when treachery allowed Parliamentary forces to enter the Castle – after which it was looted, its walls pulled down and its towers blown up.

Corfe Castle in the mist.

Corfe Castle from the village.

OPPOSITE PAGE TOP LEFT Creech Grange. The estate was originally a grange or granary of Bindon Abbey, near Wool. In 1691 the house and estate were bought by the Bond family, one of whom lost a fortune laying out the London street that bears his name.

OPPOSITE PAGE TOP RIGHT Grange Arch, Grange Hill, was built as a folly by Denis Bond in about 1740, and was intended as an 'eye-catcher' of castle battlements when seen from Creech Grange, his home in the valley below.

OPPOSITE PAGE BOTTOM A steam train of the Swanage Railway at Harman's Cross. The 11 mile Wareham to Swanage line opened in 1885 and closed in 1972, when the track was lifted. Three years later a team of volunteers formed the Swanage Railway Society, turning the disused station at Swanage into their base. Since then buildings have been restored, track relaid, engines and coaches acquired, and the line itself reopened. A ride on the Swanage Railway is one of Purbeck's most popular attractions. The Railway has a fine museum in the converted Goods Shed at Corfe Castle.

ABOVE Wild garlic and bluebells in Hyde Wood, near Steeple.

OPPOSITE PAGE TOP Looking east towards the distant blue
haze of Poole Harbour from Creech Barrow Hill. The hamlet
of East Creech lies in the shelter of Knowle Hill and the
Purbeck ridge. The fertile soils in this narrow belt of country,
squeezed between the clay of the heath and chalk of the hill,
have been farmed since at least Roman times, and remains of
a villa and other buildings have been found.

OPPOSITE PAGE BOTTOM The distant silhouette of Corfe
Castle frames the only gap in the Purbeck Hills, with Bradle
Farm on the left.

LEFT The Stars and Stripes on the flag of the United States
have their origins in the coat of arms of the Lawrence family
in St Michael's church, Steeple, where they can be seen cut in
stone in the porch, or in scarlet paint on the barrel roof. The
Lawrences were related to George Washington's family, who
wore their arms on a signet ring, which he then copied when
as first President of the newly formed Republic he designed its
flag.

ABOVE Post Office Row and the deserted village of Tyneham, with the medieval church of St Mary just visible amongst the trees in the background. In 1943 the entire village was evacuated and taken over by the War Department. When the villagers left they pinned a note to the church door: 'Please treat the church and houses with care; we have given up our homes where many of us have lived for generations to help win the war to keep men free. We shall return one day and thank you for treating the village kindly.' The Government went back on its word. In 1948 the entire village was compulsorily purchased, and it now sits inside a 7,500 acre Army firing range. Shelling, neglect and vandalism have all but destroyed it. Despite the conversion of the church and school into museums, and the thriving wildlife on the ranges, an air of sadness haunts the village and its roofless cottages.

LEFT The old school at Tyneham, as it would have been in Victorian times.

RIGHT Moving sheep on the lane to Kimmeridge. Beyond the tiny Corfe River in the valley lies Blackmanston Farm, once an Elizabethan manor house.

BELOW The Purbecks from West Creech Hill. The chalk cliffs of the Isle of Wight are just visible in the background, over 20 miles away.

ABOVE Clavell Tower, overlooking Kimmeridge Bay. The tower originally stood on the edge of the cliff and was built in 1831 by John Richards, the owner of nearby Smedmore House, probably as an observatory and seamark. For a while it was used as a coastguard's look-out, finally becoming roofless, derelict and in danger of falling victim to the gradual erosion of the cliff. In 2006, The Landmark Trust, working with a small local charity and with help from the Heritage Lottery Fund, began the painstaking task of taking down the tower, labelling each of its 16,000 stones, and moving it 25 yards inland, where it was rebuilt as holiday accommodation.

ABOVE LEFT Smedmore House, Kimmeridge. The manor was bought by William Wyot from the de Smedmores in 1391, and it has remained associated with the Wyots ever since, passing through marriage or inheritance to the Mansels, who live in it still. The bow-fronted Georgian façade conceals the remains of the house built in about 1620 by Sir William Clavell, who bankrupted himself trying to extract alum from the nearby cliffs and setting up a glass works fuelled by Kimmeridge shale.

LEFT Kimmeridge Bay is the site of an underwater Marine Wildlife Reserve. As well as a live underwater camera the Fine Foundation Marine Centre has wonderful displays on the various habitats and their wildlife.

A winter storm in Brandy Bay, with Kimmeridge Bay and the Clavell Tower visible beyond the headland.

Tumbledown dry stone walling near Gad Cliff, whose jagged limestone outcrop is 430 feet above the sea below.

LEFT The secluded beach at Arish Mell with Flowers Barrow and Worbarrow Bay in the background. Much of the Iron Age hillfort on the summit of Flowers Barrow has collapsed into the sea, but the remains of huts as well as slingstones and pottery fragments have been found within its ramparts. Inland lies Monastery Farm, where at the time of the French Revolution Thomas Weld of nearby Lulworth built a small monastery of cob and thatch as a place of refuge for a group of French monks.

OPPOSITE PAGE BOTTOM Mupe Rocks, with Worbarrow Bay beyond.

BELOW The Fossil Forest, just east of Lulworth Cove. Dorset's fossil record stretches back over 200 million years to the start of the Jurassic period, and the entire Purbeck coast is part of the UNESCO Jurassic Coast World Heritage Site. Fossilised bones of crocodiles and huge marine and flying reptiles, such as the pliosaur and pterosaur, are not uncommon, whilst at Keat's Quarry near Swanage the footprints of a dinosaur have been uncovered. Trees once stood within the hollow bowls of the Fossil Forest, marking a time when much of Dorset was a warm shallow swamp.

Lulworth Cove. The semi-circular bay is the most famous in Dorset, though because of its depth its waters are supposedly the coldest in the county. It also makes for a poor anchorage when the wind is in the south and a swell builds up in its mouth. The cove was formed when the sea broke through the hard Portland limestone cliff, eroding out the softer sands and clays and forming a high chalk cliff at the back.

The paddle steamer *Waverley* entering Lulworth Cove. The 693 ton *Waverley* was built in 1947 to replace the original, which was sunk off Dunkirk in 1940. By 1974 it seemed doomed for the breaker's yard, but was bought for £1 by the Paddle Steamer Preservation Society, and following a major restoration and refit by 2003 it had been returned to its original glory, and now sails right round Britain during the summer season.

Canoeists in the Stairhole, west of Lulworth Cove.

A jousting tournament at Lulworth Castle. The castle was probably started by Thomas, 3rd Lord Howard of Bindon, at the start of the 17th century. Despite its battlements and defensive appearance, it was intended as a hunting lodge to entertain James I when he was hunting in the Purbecks. In 1641 it was acquired by the Weld family, who own it still, but by the end of the Civil War it had been ransacked, and its contents removed. Following the Restoration in 1660, Humphrey Weld embarked on the castle's restoration and it remained the family home of the Welds until 1929, when it was gutted by fire. Recently it has been reroofed and made safe, and a small exhibition tells the story of the house and the Welds.

An oak tree's branches shade the triangular green at Coombe Keynes, where thatch, brick and local heathstone give the village its character. The sign is to the now redundant church, which, apart from the original medieval tower, was designed by the Dorchester architect John Hicks in 1861, for whom the 21-year-old Thomas Hardy was then working.

My favourite bay in Dorset, Man o' War Cove.

Dungy Head and St Oswald's Bay. The milder coastal climate combines with the thin chalk soil to make the Purbeck coast a botanist's delight. As well as the valerian in the photograph, there are orchids and specialist clifftop plants such as seakale.

One of Dorset's most famous views, Durdle Door. Its name comes from the Old English for 'pierced', after the hole in the arch.

The evening sun setting over Portland, with Durdle Door in the foreground. The little offshore rock, known as The Bull, is one of four along this section of coast; the others being The Blind Cow, The Cow, and The Calf.

Walkers enjoying the view looking east towards Durdle Door from the summit of Bat's Head.